W9-BKK-534

THE WORLD now lies divided not amongst political or geographic boundaries but amongst **financial** ones. Wealth is power, and that power rests with only a handful of **FAMILIES**.

The few who provide a service to their ruling Family are cared for and protected.

All others are **Waste**.

———

The Families are at **WAR**.
The Lazari of **BITTNER**, **MORRAY**, and **ARMITAGE** pursue the ultimate destruction of **RAUSLING** and the liberation of Western Europe.

While the **CARLYLE FAMILY** has troops on the ground, they have no Lazarus to field. **FOREVER CARLYLE** is recovering from grievous injuries suffered during the Battle of Duluth. Worse, her doubts about her Family have left her faith in tatters, and her trust in ruins.

Now **JOHANNA CARLYLE**, acting Head of the Family, must make a dangerous choice. Does she obey her father, **Malcolm Carlyle**, and continue to chain Forever with chemicals and lies; or does she tell Forever the truth?

And to the east, the **DRAGON** stirs from its slumber....

LAZARUS

IMAGE COMICS, INC.
Robert Kirkman—**Chief Operating Officer**
Erik Larsen—**Chief Financial Officer**
Todd McFarlane—**President**
Marc Silvestri—**Chief Executive Officer**
Jim Valentino—**Vice-President**

Eric Stephenson—**Publisher**
Corey Murphy—**Director of Sales**
Jeff Boison—**Director of Publishing Planning & Book Trade Sales**
Chris Ross—**Director of Digital Sales**
Jeff Stang—**Director of Specialty Sales**
Kat Salazar—**Director of PR & Marketing**
Branwyn Bigglestone—**Controller**
Sue Korpela—**Accounts Manager**
Drew Gill—**Art Director**
Brett Warnock—**Production Manager**
Meredith Wallace—**Print Manager**
Tricia Ramos—**Traffic Manager**
Briah Skelly—**Publicist**
Aly Hoffman—**Events & Conventions Coordinator**
Sasha Head—**Sales & Marketing Production Designer**
David Brothers—**Branding Manager**
Melissa Gifford—**Content Manager**
Drew Fitzgerald—**Publicity Assistant**
Vincent Kukua—**Production Artist**
Erika Schnatz—**Production Artist**
Ryan Brewer—**Production Artist**
Shanna Matuszak—**Production Artist**
Carey Hall—**Production Artist**
Esther Kim—**Direct Market Sales Representative**
Emilio Bautista—**Digital Sales Representative**
Leanna Caunter—**Accounting Assistant**
Chloe Ramos-Peterson—**Library Market Sales Representative**
Marla Eizik—**Administrative Assistant**
IMAGECOMICS.COM

LAZARUS, VOLUME FIVE: CULL

First printing. May 2017. Published by Image Comics, Inc. Office of publication: 2701 NW Vaughn St., Suite 780, Portland, OR 97210. Copyright © 2017 Greg Rucka and Michael Lark. All rights reserved.

Contains material originally published in single magazine form as LAZARUS #22-26. "Lazarus," its logos, and the likenesses of all characters herein are trademarks of Greg Rucka and Michael Lark, unless otherwise noted.

"Image" and the Image Comics logos are registered trademarks of Image Comics, Inc. No part of this publication may be reproduced or transmitted, in any form or by any means (except for short excerpts for journalistic or review purposes), without the express written permission of Greg Rucka, Michael Lark, or Image Comics, Inc. All names, characters, events, and locales in this publication are entirely fictional. Any resemblance to actual persons (living or dead), events, or places, without satiric intent, is coincidental. Printed in the USA. For information regarding the CPSIA on this printed material call: 203-595-3636 and provide reference #RICH–736908.

For international rights, contact: foreignlicensing@imagecomics.com.

ISBN: 978-1-5343-0024-8